Shoes

and

Other Footwear

Jane Bingham

WAYLAND

First published in 2008 by Wayland

Copyright © Wayland 2008

Wayland
Hachette Children's Books
338 Euston Road
London NW1 3BH

Wayland Australia
Level 17/207 Kent Street
Sydney NSW 2000

Senior editor: Joyce Bentley
Designer: Holly Fullbrook
Picture researcher: Kathy Lockley

British Library Cataloguing in Publication Data
Bingham, Jane
        Shoes and other footwear. - (Clothes around the world)
        1. Footwear - Juvenile literature
        I. Title
        391.4'13

ISBN 978 0 7502 5310 9

Picture acknowledgements:
Air Kicks: 1, 26
James L. Amos/Corbis: 12; Construction Photography/Alamy: 18; Jim Craigmyle/Corbis: 17
Julio Donoso/Corbis-Sygma: 5; Randy Faris/Corbis: 21; Ilian Ballet/Alamy: 22;
Image100/Corbis: 15, 23; Image Source/Corbis: 6; joeysworld.com/Alamy: 13; Lake County
Museum/Corbis: 10; Charles Platiau/Reuters/Corbis: 24; Philippe Poulet/Mission/Getty
Images: 16; Red Fred/Alamy: 3, 14; RESET/Rex Features: 25; Shotfile/Alamy: 4; Jill
Stephenson/Alamy: 27; Stephen Vidler/Eurasia Press/Corbis: 7; Visual Arts Library
(London)/Alamy: 8, 9, 11; Wayland Archive: 19, 28, 29, 30; Anthony West/Corbis: 20

Printed in China

Wayland is a division of Hachette Children's Books,
an Hachette Livre UK company.

www.hachettelivre.co.uk

Contents

Why do people wear shoes?

For thousands of years, people have worn shoes to protect their feet. Wearing shoes stops you damaging the **soles** of your feet on rough surfaces. Shoes also keep your feet warm and dry when the weather is cold and wet.

Shoes make it easier for you to walk. They help you grip the ground, and they give your feet some support.

It Works!

Sandal success
Modern **hiking** sandals are very well designed. Their thick rubber soles protect your feet from sharp stones, and stop you slipping. You can also adjust the straps to make sure that your ankles are supported.

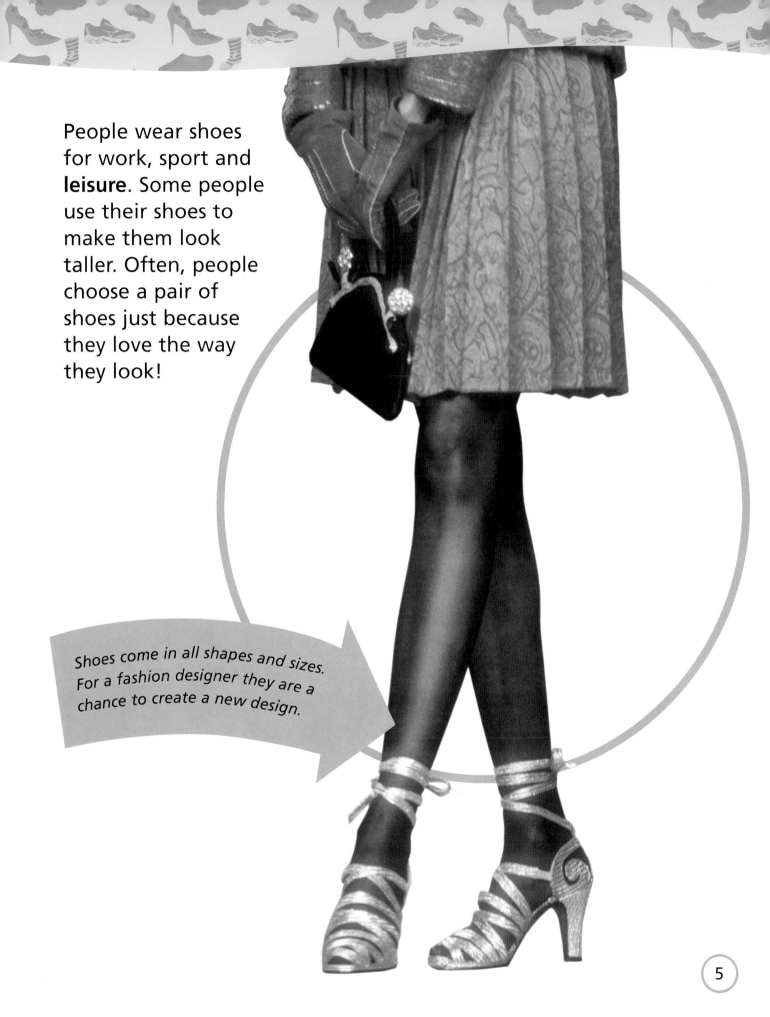

People wear shoes for work, sport and **leisure**. Some people use their shoes to make them look taller. Often, people choose a pair of shoes just because they love the way they look!

Shoes come in all shapes and sizes. For a fashion designer they are a chance to create a new design.

Shoes around the world

People around the world wear many different types of shoes. Often, their shoes are specially suited to the weather in their country.

In cold, snowy places, such as **Alaska**, people wear thick, waterproof boots. They also have wide snowshoes to help them glide over the snow. In Mexico, where it is hot and dry, people wear sandals. Mexican sandals are made from strips of **plaited** leather.

When people wear snowshoes, they can glide over the snow, instead of sinking into it.

Japanese women need to have lots of practice before they can walk easily in their geta.

What Would You Wear?

What shoes would you wear in a hot, rainy country?
A. Rope sandals
B. Wellington boots
C. Hiking sandals
D. Trainers

(Answer on page 31)

In some parts of the world, people still wear **traditional** shoes. The style of these shoes has stayed the same for hundreds of years. For example, in Japan people wear traditional sandals called **geta**. They are raised above the ground on thick wooden blocks.

The history of shoes

Thousands of years ago, people made shoes from animal skins. First, they wrapped a skin around their foot and leg. Then they tied it in place with narrow leather strips. People had to tie the strips very tightly to stop their shoes from falling off.

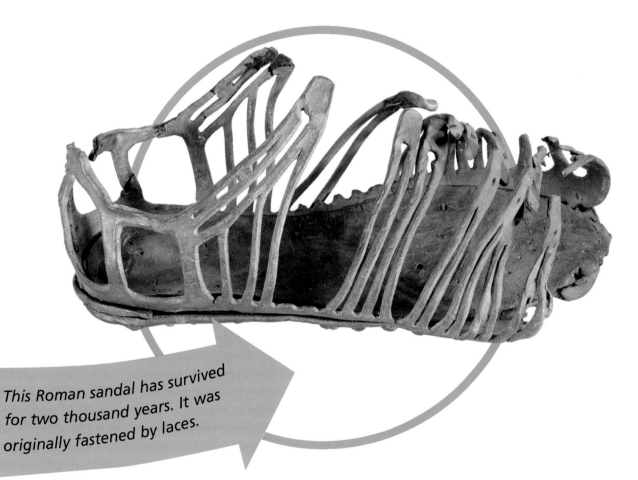

This Roman sandal has survived for two thousand years. It was originally fastened by laces.

In **roman times**, most people wore leather sandals. Roman soldiers had iron nails hammered into the soles of their sandals. This made the soles very strong, so the soldiers could march for miles.

Weird and Wonderful

Turned-up toes
In **medieval times**, it was the fashion to wear shoes with long, pointed toes. Sometimes the toes were so long that they had to be attached to the wearer's leg with a chain.

In the 1700s, wealthy people in Europe wore very fancy shoes. Men, women and children had shoes with heels. Their shoes were fastened with a silver **buckle** or a large bow.

Moose River Handicraft Moccasins

Moccasins have become popular leisure shoes, known for their design and comfort.

Native Americans made soft leather shoes called moccasins. Hunters wore moccasins when they crept silently towards their prey.

By the 1800s, fashions had changed. Adults and children wore ankle boots that were fastened by lots of buttons. Button boots were very hot to wear in summer.

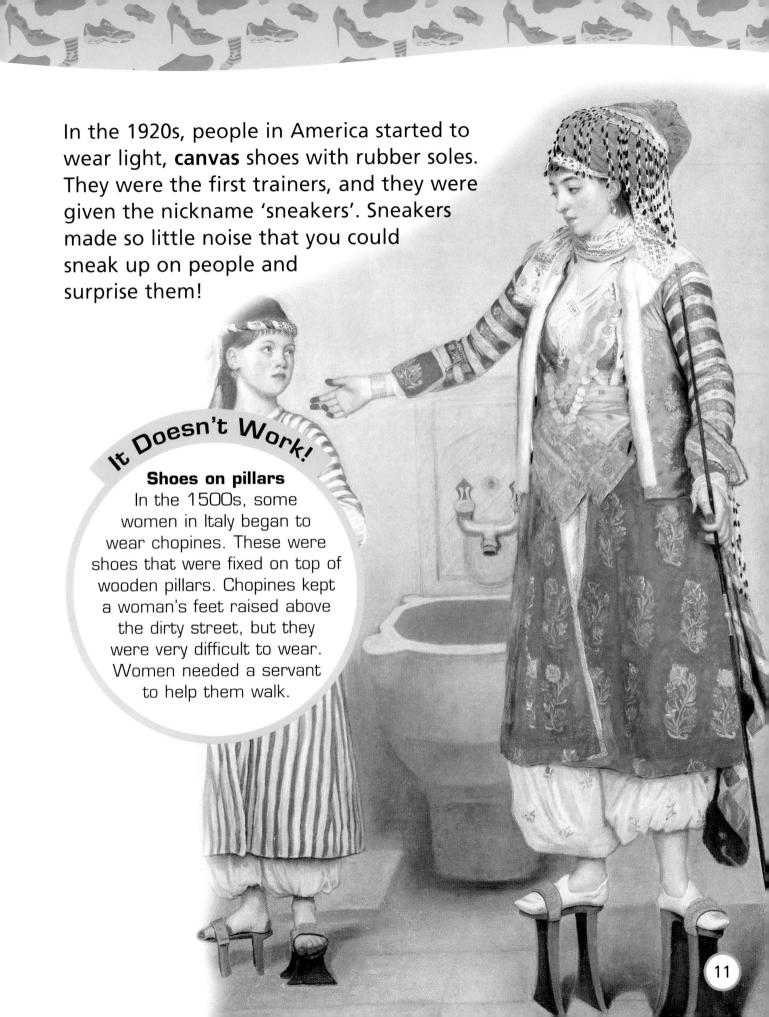

In the 1920s, people in America started to wear light, **canvas** shoes with rubber soles. They were the first trainers, and they were given the nickname 'sneakers'. Sneakers made so little noise that you could sneak up on people and surprise them!

It Doesn't Work!

Shoes on pillars
In the 1500s, some women in Italy began to wear chopines. These were shoes that were fixed on top of wooden pillars. Chopines kept a woman's feet raised above the dirty street, but they were very difficult to wear. Women needed a servant to help them walk.

What are shoes made from?

Most boots and shoes are made from leather. Leather is a very good material for shoes because it is strong but also **flexible**. Leather shoes give lots of support to your feet, but at the same time they feel soft and comfortable.

These musicians are wearing traditional wooden clogs. When they tap their feet, they make a loud sound!

In the past, many people wore clogs carved from wood. Modern clogs often have leather tops and wooden soles.

Thick **cowhide** is used to make hard-wearing boots and shoes. **Suede** is used for softer shoes. Sheepskin slippers have a thick, woolly lining that make your feet feel cosy. Some winter boots are lined with fur to give them extra comfort and warmth.

Flashback

Clogs with a difference
Traditional clogs are made from wood, which is very heavy. Now some clogs are made from rubber, which is much lighter. These rubber clogs are called Crocs. They are very comfortable to wear.

Shoes can be made from straw, grass or rope. They can be knitted from wool, or made from cotton. Nowadays, rubber and plastic are also used for making shoes.

Rubber is waterproof, and it can be moulded into any shape. It is often used for making soles, but sometimes whole shoes are moulded from rubber. Wellington boots and flip-flops are both made from rubber.

Wellington boots come in all sizes and colours. They do a great job of keeping your feet clean and dry.

Plastic is another good material for shoes. It is used to make beach shoes that can go in the water. Plastic can also be moulded into special boots for skiing and skating.

It Works!

Ski boots

Ski boots used to be made from leather, but now they are made from plastic. Plastic boots are safer than leather boots because they hold the skier's ankle very firmly. This means that fewer skiers have accidents.

Footwear for work

Some people wear special boots or shoes for work.
Farmers wear high rubber boots to protect their
legs from mud. Fishermen have lightweight boots
with a very good grip to stop them slipping on the
deck of a ship.

Weird and Wonderful

Heavy boots

Deep-sea divers wear
special boots with
heavy weights built into
them. The boots stop
the diver's legs from
floating upwards, and
they allow them to walk
on the ocean floor.

When surgeons perform an operation, their shoes need to be free from germs. Sometimes they wear rubber boots or clogs. These rubber shoes can be thoroughly washed before an operation.

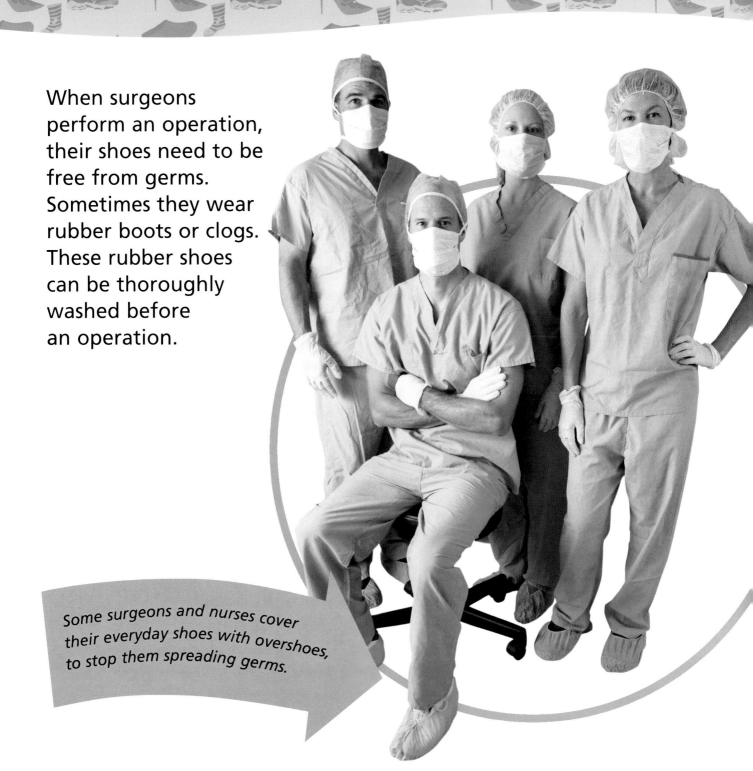

Some surgeons and nurses cover their everyday shoes with overshoes, to stop them spreading germs.

In the western states of America, cattle herders wear cowboy boots. Cowboy boots have wide legs, so the herders can tuck their trousers inside their boots, and protect their ankles from thorns and snakes.

Footwear for protection and safety

Some footwear is designed to make the wearer as safe as possible. Workers on building sites have strong work boots with thick rubber soles. The soles have deep ridges to help the wearer grip uneven ground.

Work boots have a metal toecap and a metal plate underneath the foot. The metal protects the worker's feet if something heavy falls on them, or if they step on something sharp.

Work boots have to stand up to very rough treatment. You can see the toecaps in these battered boots.

When people go rock climbing, they wear special shoes to help them stay safe. Climbers need to balance on their toes or heels, but they also need to bend their feet. Climbing shoes have very strong toes and heels, but they are also light and flexible.

What Would You Wear?

Which shoes would you choose to protect your feet if you were walking across a hot and stony desert?
A. Sandals
B. Hiking boots
C. Climbing shoes
D. Work boots
(Answer on page 31)

Climbing shoes must fit tightly and the soles need to grip the rock very well.

Footwear for sport and leisure

Many sports have their own special footwear. Sports shoes can be specially designed to help the wearer play their sport as well as possible.

Soccer boots have plastic studs on their soles to help the player grip the ground. Some boots even have studs for different surfaces. Longer studs give extra grip on wet, muddy ground. Shorter studs are used for dry, hard ground.

It Works!

Keeping feet fit

When people go training they wear special trainers. Running trainers have thick rubber soles to reduce the **impact** of the runner's foot hitting the ground. They also have built-in pads to support the runner's ankles and heels.

Rollerboots are made from strong plastic that give the feet and ankles lots of support. The shape of the boots allow the skater to lean forward and bend at the knees. This is the safest position for rollerskating.

Ice skates need to be laced up tightly to give the skater's ankles lots of support.

Ballet shoes have blocks fitted into the end of the toes. Ballerinas wear special ballet shoes for dancing on their toes. These shoes have soft blocks that support the dancer's toes.

Tap shoes have metal plates on their soles and heels. The plates make a loud tapping sound when the dancer's foot hits the floor.

When a ballerina dances in ballet shoes, her legs look very long and graceful.

When people are relaxing at home, they like to wear comfortable leisure shoes. Trainers and flip-flops are popular choices for leisurewear.

Flashback

Flip-flops from Japan

For hundreds of years, Japanese women and girls have worn simple sandals, known as zori. Zori have a lightweight sole made from straw, and two cotton straps with a **thong** between the toes. In the 1940s, people in America copied the style of Japanese zori. They made simple sandals with thongs. But the sandals were made from rubber instead of straw.

Fashion shoes

Fashion designers create some amazing shoes. They try out different styles until they come up with something new.

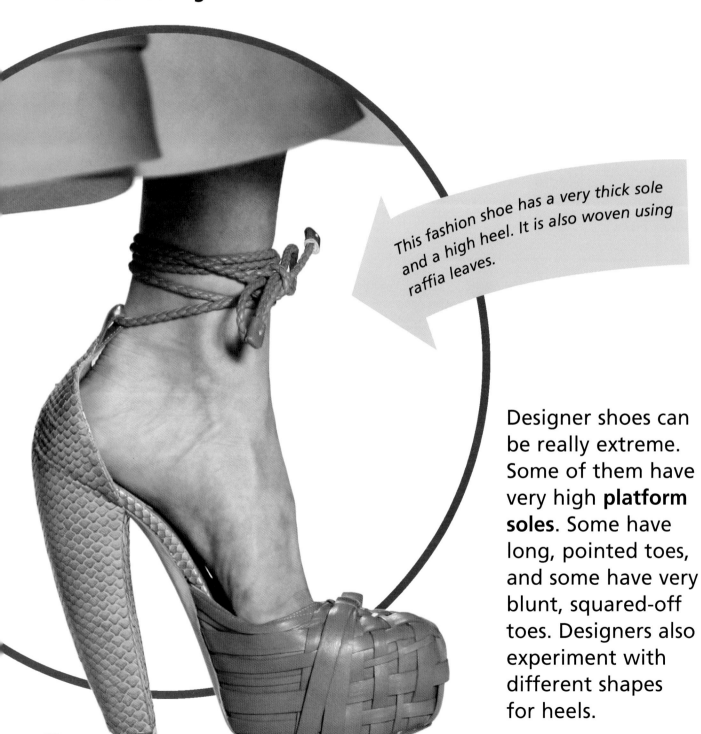

This fashion shoe has a very thick sole and a high heel. It is also woven using raffia leaves.

Designer shoes can be really extreme. Some of them have very high **platform soles**. Some have long, pointed toes, and some have very blunt, squared-off toes. Designers also experiment with different shapes for heels.

Fashion designers use a range of materials for their shoes. Some fashion shoes are made from clear plastic. When models wear these shoes, they look as if their feet are floating on air!

It Doesn't Work!

Extra high heels
Very high, narrow heels are known as stilettos. It is very hard to balance on these heels, and women can have some nasty falls. Stiletto heels sink into soft ground and they can even get stuck in drains in the road!

Shoes for fun

Shoes don't have to be sensible. They can come in a range of vivid colours. They can be covered in fantastic patterns. They can even look like furry animals!

Some childrens' shoes have patterns on their soles, that leave amazing footprints. Some have built-in lights that flash when you walk. There are also shoes with roller-wheels in their soles, so you can rollerskate when you get tired of walking.

Weird and Wonderful

Bouncy boots
Some boots have special soles that act like trampolines. So, when you walk in them, you bounce! These special boots make you take large, bouncing steps, rather like a spaceman walking on the moon.

People have been having fun with footwear for years. In medieval times, **jesters** wore shoes with bells on the end of the toes.

Clowns wear enormous shoes that flap around when they walk. What crazy shoes would you like to wear?

A pair of giant shoes are an important part of a clown's outfit.

Make your own moccasins

Moccasins are soft leather shoes that were first worn by Native Americans. Some moccasins had a hard sole to protect the feet from rough ground, soft soles were used where the ground was gentler. Your shoes don't have strong leather soles, so you can only wear them indoors.

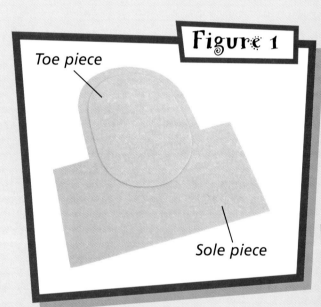

Figure 1

Toe piece

Sole piece

1. Cut out two pieces of felt, as shown in figure 1. The toe piece should be 2 cm wider than your foot.

Figure 2

2. Fold the sole piece in half with the straight sides of the felt together. Sew up the heel edge with a running stitch, 1.5cm from the edge. Turn back and sew between the stitches already sewn.

Figure 3

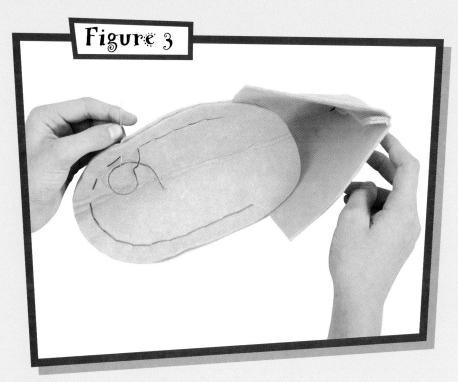

3. Turn the sole piece inside out so the stitching is on the inside. Now use running stitches to sew the toe piece on to the sole piece. Stop sewing when you reach the taller part of the sole piece and leave a gap at the top.

4. Thread a cord with beads and feathers. Loop the cord around the heel, and knot it loosely at the front. Turn down the sides and the front of the shoe. Now repeat steps 1 to 4 to make the other moccasin.

Figure 4

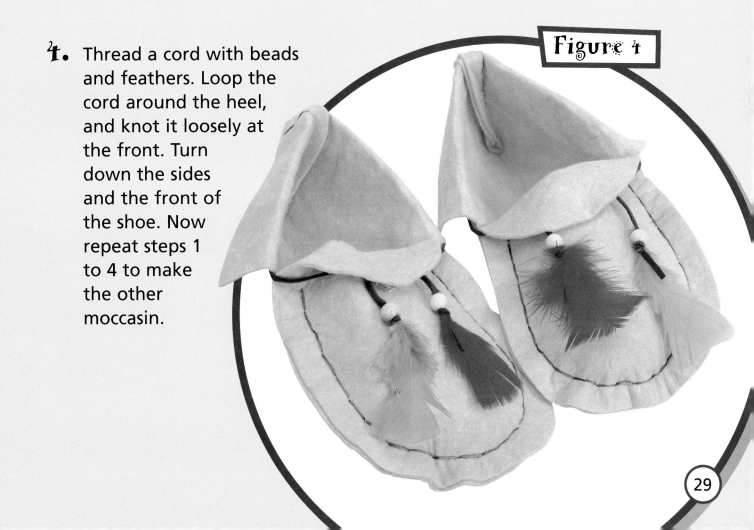

Dress-up box

5-minute clown

Clowns wear very big trousers and a giant shirt. They have very long, flapping shoes, and they often wear a silly hat.

To create your costume, you will need some big trousers and a shirt, two pairs of adult's socks, and some colourful scarves or ties. Some face paints and a hat will add to the effect.

He he he!

1. First, make your clown shoes by rolling two of the socks into a ball. Then, push the rolled-up balls into the toes of the other two socks.

2. Next, put on your trousers and shirt, and tie a scarf around your neck.

3. Put your foot inside one of the socks, so the rolled-up ball rests on your toes. Wind a tie round your foot a few times, and tie the ends in a bow.

4. Do the same for the other foot. Add face paints and a hat and get ready to clown around!

Glossary

Alaska – a part of North America where it is very cold and snowy

buckle – a metal fastening on shoes or clothes

canvas – very strong, thick cotton

cowhide – strong, thick leather from a cow

flexible – able to bend easily

geta – Japanese shoes with a high wooden sole and a thong between the toes

hiking – walking in the countryside

impact – the action of one thing hitting another

jester – someone who entertained people in medieval times, by making jokes

leisure – free time when you do not have to work

medieval times – a period of history between the years 1000 and 1450

plaited – twisted together

platform sole – an extremely thick sole for a shoe

rollerboots – boots with wheels in their soles that are used for rollerskating

roman times – a period of history from B.C 31 – A.D. 28

sole – the underneath part of a foot or a shoe

suede – soft leather with a smooth, velvet-like surface

thong – a strap on a shoe or sandal that goes between the big toe and the second toe

traditional – used in the same way for hundreds of years

What would you wear?

Answers to questions on pages 7 and 19.

Page 7
The best choice of shoes to wear in a hot and rainy country would be C – hiking sandals. Rope sandals would soon get soggy in the rain, and your feet would be much too hot and sweaty in wellington boots. Trainers would be the next best choice, but after a while they would get soggy and sweaty too!

Page 19
If you were walking across a hot and stony desert you'd be best off wearing B – hiking boots. If you wore sandals, you'd stub your toes on the rocks. Climbing shoes would bend too much, and you'd feel the sharp stones under your feet. If you chose work boots, the metal toecaps and sole plates would soon get burning hot.

Index

Photos or pictures are shown below in bold, **like this**.